# REAL RISK

# MANAGEMENT

## For the Electrical Grid

*Competent Risk Management*
*Based on Authoritative Threat Assessments*

The Real Risk Management Series: *Monograph 1*
Local Critical Task Planning for Long-Term Blackouts

## By Jim LeBlanc

For more information about this book, visit
SECUREFREEDOM.ORG

Real Risk Management is published in the United States by the Center for Security Policy Press, a division of the Center for Security Policy.

ISBN-13: 978-1533122377

ISBN-10: 1533122377

The Center for Security Policy
1901 Pennsylvania Avenue, NW, Suite 201
Washington, D.C. 20006
Phone: 202-835-9077
Email: info@SecureFreedom.org
For more information, visit SecureFreedom.org

# Contents

Introduction to The Real Risk Management Series ................................ 1

Foreword ................................................................................ 9

Acknowledgments ...................................................................... 10

Purpose................................................................................. 10

Surviving an Electromagnetic Pulse (EMP) Event................................ 11

Electromagnetic Pulse (EMP)........................................................ 12

Event Horizon Timelines ............................................................ 15

Critical Planning Elements.......................................................... 15

    *Books/Knowledge* ............................................................ 16

    *Water* ....................................................................... 18

    *Food* ......................................................................... 22

    *Clothing* ..................................................................... 26

    *Sanitation* ................................................................... 28

    *Shelter* ...................................................................... 29

    *First Aid/Medical* ........................................................... 30

    *Communications* ............................................................ 35

    *Alternative Power Sources* ................................................. 43

    *Transportation* .............................................................. 48

Miscellaneous......................................................................... 52

Epilogue............................................................................... 55

# INTRODUCTION TO
## The Real Risk Management Series

The Center for Security Policy (CSP) released a publication entitled *Guilty Knowledge: What the U.S. Government Knows about the Vulnerability of the Electric Grid, But Refuses to Fix* in 2013. The title is rightly provocative, and it contains executive summaries and excerpts from eleven authoritative government studies on known threats and vulnerabilities regarding the U.S. electric grid including:

- Global Trends 2030[1] is from the office of the Director on National Intelligence (*required reading for the intelligence community*), and it describes a "hostile electromagnetic or radiated environment. In this instance, nuclear first use would not be used to harm humans as much as to deny opponents use of electronic systems."

- The Congressional Commission on the Strategic Posture of the United States[2]

- Terrorism and the Electric Power Delivery System[3] (2012) Committee on Enhancing the Robustness and Resilience of Future Electrical Transmission and Distribution in the United States to Terrorist Attack; Board on Energy and Environmental Systems; Division on Engineering and Physical Sciences; National Research Council

- Intentional Electromagnetic Interference (IEMI) and Its Impact on the U.S. Power Grid,[4] Oak Ridge National Laboratory

- Electromagnetic Pulse: Effects on the U.S. Power Grid,[5] Federal Energy Regulatory Commission

- Severe Space Weather Events,[6] National Research Council of the National Academies

---

[1] http://www.dni.gov/files/documents/GlobalTrends_2030.pdf
[2] http://media.usip.org/reports/strat_posture_report.pdf
[3] http://www.nap.edu/openbook.php?record_id=12050
[4] http://www.ferc.gov/industries/electric/indus-act/reliability/cybersecurity/ferc_meta-r-323.pdf
[5] http://www.ferc.gov/industries/electric/indus-act/reliability/cybersecurity/ferc_meta-r-323.pdf
[6] http://www.nap.edu/openbook.php?record_id=12507

- The EMP Commission,[7] The Commission to Assess the Threat to the United States from Electromagnetic Pulse

This particular vulnerability is technologically unique because our current grid system is so interconnected that a variety of different threats can take down large parts of America's power supply. A single attack would be less likely to cause long-term blackouts if U.S. electric power supplies were local and diverse. Those threats to the nation's grid include cyber-attacks; physical attacks to key substations; solar storms; and, high altitude nuclear detonations. These types of attacks do not directly cause a threat to human life because the target is infrastructure rather than people. However, the secondary effects of power loss over time do affect people, causing catastrophic losses of life over weeks and months.

From a national security perspective, it is the asymmetric nature of the vulnerabilities described above that makes the electrical grid a desirable target for terrorist organizations and hostile countries. Mitigating vulnerabilities minimizes targets. It changes our enemies' evaluation of U.S. infrastructure weakness and impacts their cost-benefit calculation in developing their capability to take down our electrical grid.

In terms of man-caused threats, this means protecting the grid is a matter of taking the target off of our backs and denying a kill shot capability to jihadis, rogue countries, and even state sponsored cyber armies. No mitigation, however, can deter solar weather.

CSP formed the Secure the Grid Coalition to bring together a cross section of scientists, engineers, intelligence professionals, and national security policy experts to enhance insights about electrical grid vulnerability by bridging gaps across their respective disciplines. Among these security experts are emergency planners from a group of private sector and local law enforcement professionals called InfraGard; they partner with the FBI to share information and intelligence to prevent hostile acts against the U.S.

*The Real Risk Management Series* is being introduced to show what emergency planners and other groups on a local level are doing to take responsibility where they can when the government and industry fail to fill

---

[7]    http://empcommission.org

the security gap. A security gap occurs when government, and in this case industry, fail to adapt legally and through security measures to a new threat environment.

The goal of the local level emergency planner, who understands the new threat environment, is to prepare their local community for a long-term blackout that may be caused by a solar storm; cyber-attack; system wide asymmetric rogue element, person, or country; or terrorist attack that takes down most of the U.S. electric grid.

Are we really at risk of these types of attack? The answer is YES. To learn more about the vulnerability of the U.S. electric grid and why this monograph and this series are so vitally important, visit www.securethegrid.com.

The government assesses that a long-term blackout (4-12 months or more) would cause between 60 to 90 percent loss of life in the United States due to interruption of operations or destruction of critical infrastructures: access to food; clean water; obliteration of communication systems; and a breakdown in society and the rule of law.

It is important to keep in mind that long-term blackouts are preventable. Affordable technology exists that can protect the current electric grid. The failure to implement these mitigations is a testament to crippling bureaucracy in the government, but more importantly, resistance to government regulation by a technologically outdated electric industry.

The technological monopoly created by electric utility lobbies is the reason this vulnerability prevails. If electric generation had developed in a truly free market in America, innovators would compete to create local decentralized sources of power that could more easily recover from catastrophic events on a local level. For example, based on the current electric grid, a system failure in Ohio can deprive people in New England from life sustaining power supplies. The interconnectedness of the electrical grid is a crucial element that makes America so vulnerable. The resistance to safety regulations by the electrical utility industry is what compounds this vulnerability.

It is essential in securing the grid to approach systemic resolution in both short-term and long-term perspectives. In the short-term, neutral ground blocking devices on critical High Voltage Transformers, blocking capacitors on key nodes of our power lines, and the type of protection the U.S. military already uses on its critical assets need to be applied appropriately to critical components of the civilian electric infrastructure. In the long-term, our future electrical generation system needs to grow from competitive innovation with security and resilience integral to the design.

A logical question is: "If the military knows about these threats and have protected their key assets, why hasn't the nation's MOST critical infrastructure — the electric grid — been protected?" The answer: Our government and the electric industry do not practice *REAL RISK MANAGEMENT*. So, what is *Real Risk Management*, and why don't we have it now?

One of the major findings of the Center for Security Policy in its examination of the government's failure to abate such a seemingly simple vulnerability has to do with authority. Many good faith efforts have been made by the Executive Branch, including the Department of Homeland Security, the White House Office of Science and Technology Policy, and Congress, to urge the electric utility industry to protect its critical assets from a wide array of threats in the same way the U.S. military has been protecting strategic nuclear forces and command-and-control facilities for decades.

Under current law and electric industry regulatory structures, the U.S. government does not have the authority to force the industry to harden its assets against well-documented, well-researched threats. Why? Because the electric utility industry is our nation's last self-regulated industry and it has been wildly successful in protecting that status.

The U.S. government *does* expend a significant amount of time, manpower, and money to protect the nation's critical infrastructure. However, because the electric utility industry does not have a government safety regulator equivalent to something like the Federal Aviation Administration, which enforces proper regulation of the airline industry to ensure the safety of Americans aboard aircraft, government efforts always fail to actually fix the electric grid's vulnerabilities. As a comparison, imagine the FAA composed of executives from major airlines with the authority to write the rules for airline safety and then have those rules approved by a federal agency staffed with former airline industry executives and employees.

The National Protection and Programs Directorate at the Department of Homeland Security (NPPD) is an example of the federal government's well-meaning but less-than-effective attempts to protect infrastructure. The NPPD's mission is to protect the nation's physical and cyber infrastructure. Under the NPPD, the National Cyber and Communications Integration Center is a major cyber threat-monitoring program that works with industry to protect the control systems of critical infrastructures from cyber-attacks that have physical consequences.

In a 2014 interview with CNN, NPPD director Susan Spalding explained that most of those critical infrastructures are owned by the private sector, not by the government, and that "the private sector has a responsibility and we do everything we can to assist them."[8] That perfectly summarizes the relationship and the legal authoritative line the government will not cross. It is an admission the government can do a lot to help, but the private sector has the responsibility.

Under the current system for the grid, the electric industry can point to the NPPD and say the government has the national security component well in hand. The electric industry then has the government on the hook for the electric industry's security costs and responsibilities.

To perpetuate such an arrangement, electric utility lobbyists have developed several memes that have become unwritten laws in the government tactic. The most common is the *public-private partnership* approach. The government accepts that, as major stakeholders, the private electric utility industry should have a large degree of control and buy-in on the creation and implementation of safety standards.

The inability of electrical utility systems to recover from a system-wide failure raises questions about the effectiveness of this approach. At this moment, no public electrical utility has developed a realistic restart capability for a system-wide failure caused by a nuclear electromagnetic pulse (EMP) attack or solar super storm. This is despite the many exercises

---

[8] Feyerick, Deborah. "Cybersecurity: Is Our Infrastructure Safe?" CNN. December 8, 2014. Accessed October 8, 2015. http://www.cnn.com/TRANSCRIPTS/1412/08/sn.01.html

and programs they have conducted to demonstrate they are doing something to protect their assets.

What they are really protecting themselves from is liability costs. This justified concern to insulate from liability comes from having created artificially low safety standards.

Electrical utility lobbyists down play the imminent danger facing people in America. They aim to avoid unwanted scrutiny of the security gap created by the public-private partnership when members of Congress or the Executive Branch express concern about threats to the electrical grid including enemy attacks, recurring solar super storms and high altitude EMP attacks (HEMP).

The National Intelligence Council claimed in their 2012 publication *Global Trends 2030*, "solar geomagnetic storms could knock out satellites, the electric grid, and many sensitive electronic devices. The recurrence intervals of crippling solar geomagnetic storms, which are less than a century, now pose a substantial threat because of the world's dependence on electricity."

Through the successful placement of industry-connected political appointees, the electric utility lobby has conditioned DHS and the Department of Energy to treat threats in this category, which are labeled *High Impact Low Frequency* events, in accordance with what they call a "Risk Management" approach. In this Risk Management approach, high frequency events regardless of impact are given priority.

Bureaucrats and electric utilities absolve themselves of responsibility for mitigating solar storms by saying they don't happen often. Often isn't the issue. It's a matter of certitude: the occurrence of a solar super storm striking earth is a mathematical certainty based on historical documentation and timing.

Compounding such folly, the electrical utility lobby might conflate *do they or don't they* threat types, such as the mathematical probability of a solar storm and an assessment of North Korea's EMP attack capability, for example. A proper threat assessment of an EMP attack launched from a satellite or a clandestine ocean freighter is in a completely different category than calculations based on solar observation data. Conflating the two is irresponsible.

National security threats from hostile actors like North Korea and Iran are not a matter of mathematical probability. They are based on capability and intent, much like the cyber threat to the electrical grid from China and Russia. NSA director Admiral Michael S. Rogers testified before Congress that the Chinese are conducting cyber-attacks against our electrical grid and will soon have the capability to take it down.

When the U.S. government identifies a hostile capability and/or a hostile intent, it traditionally takes defensive measures. Those who promote the Risk Management approach argue that because EMP attacks and solar storms happen infrequently, they should be at the bottom of the list for managing risks.

It is infrequent that Jihadists fly airplanes into buildings, but the government still employs tens of thousands of people to screen Americans in airports to guard against this "low probability" event. Meanwhile, our nation's adversaries — and Mother Nature — threaten catastrophic harm to our nation's most critical infrastructure, whose loss would kill 9 out of 10 Americans in less than 12 months. Remarkably, those responsible for the infrastructure prevent it from being protected.

It is this disconnect that prompted the creation of *The Real Risk Management Series.* As CSP continues to provide expert analysis on threats to our nation's critical grid infrastructure, it will also seek to identify those individuals, organizations, and governments who are managing risks in a logical and strategic response to the government's own assessment of the threats and vulnerabilities.

The British government realized the dire threat from geomagnetic solar storms and released its Space Weather Preparedness Strategy in July 2015. Their strategy document has a section for local preparedness and an assessment of what the British government has done and still needs to do. Similar efforts have begun in the White House office of Science and Technology Policy with its own Space Weather Strategy document released in 2015, which was followed by a Space Weather Action Plan.

Unfortunately this initial effort suffers the same "public-private partnership" and "risk management" approaches that have hindered past attempts to protect the electric grid. It may, however, succeed in highlighting the need for national level planning scenarios for long-term blackouts like those the British government produced. It also challenges electrical utilities to use existing data as a way of pushing back on tactics to procrastinate with promises of more studies that take years to conduct. It is not a legal document promising real accountability, but it is a positive step toward a more candid culture regarding the threat of space weather.

While we can find some encouragement in recent positive steps taken by the White House, *Real Risk Management* would mean using the tools we have now to mitigate the risks we have long known about.

Many Americans are asking, "What can I do?"

The Center for Security Policy recommends that citizens educate themselves on the vulnerability of the U.S. electric grid and become active in the fight to harden it with an "all hazards" approach. At the same time the Center encourages emergency planners to begin planning for long-term blackouts — both as a means to protect the lives of fellow citizens and to drive home the gravity of America's current vulnerability.

Future monographs will focus on companies, industries, and governments as part of the *Real Risk Management* series because more than just families and local communities need resources available to conduct Real Risk Management, emergency preparedness planning, and effective defense of critical infrastructure.

Additionally, and perhaps most importantly, CSP will continue its efforts to educate Americans and policymakers on the vulnerability and importance of *Securing the Grid*. These efforts will continue to be chronicled at its website: www.securethegrid.com.

# Foreword

The Center for Security Policy is proud to work with Jim LeBlanc, an emergency planner who provides in these pages what the government has not yet done in an emergency preparedness document. That is to apply *Real Risk Management* by collecting and prioritizing emergency preparedness best practices for families and local communities to survive a long-term blackout.

Jim is Vice President of the New Orleans Chapter of the InfraGard Louisiana Members Alliance, an information sharing alliance between the FBI and the private sector, and owns Contingency Planning Consultants, LLC. He has an undergraduate degree from the University of New Orleans and a Master's in Business Administration from Pepperdine University. He served as the Chief Financial Officer for a chemical company for 23 years and also served as a Reserve Deputy for his local sheriff's office for 8 years.

He is part of a growing trend of national security practitioners outside the U.S. government and electrical utility industry who are taking action to help their own communities based on our nation's best threat assessments. His expertise and experience in this field provide the opportunity for this monograph to outline, in detail, effective planning measures we can exercise to prepare ourselves and our families for life without power.

Nick Hanlon
Critical Infrastructure Security
Project Manager
Center for Security Policy

# Acknowledgments

This monograph was possible with the gracious assistance of a large group of individuals who donated their knowledge and time to developing this book to help people survive in a grid-down post-EMP/CME event environment. These individuals include Nicholas Hanlon, Tommy Waller, Dr. George Baker, Lester Millet, Chris Laborde, Eric Pickering, Jerry Emanuelson, Glenn Rhoades, Henry Newton and some of the groups they represent. Thank you to many others for their assistance and input, and we also recognize the many websites referenced for their vast contributions.

# Purpose

This monograph was created with the explicit intent of providing guidance to the individual or family on surviving without electricity for a very long period of time (i.e., "Living off the Grid"). It is not meant as a "how to do" as much as it is a "what to do before."

Another purpose for this manual is to underscore the need for policymakers at the local, state, and federal level to SECURE the electric grid. **Therefore, part of the personal survival plan should include working to impel our leaders to take essential actions to secure our grid.**

Those "survivalists" and "preppers" who have given up on their leaders in Washington and in their particular states must remember that the founders of this nation didn't retreat from problems — they faced them head on. One of the most important aspects of "what to do before" is to work to SECURE THE GRID. You can learn more about this effort at www.securethegrid.com.

# Surviving an Electromagnetic Pulse (EMP) Event

An EMP or a coronal mass ejection (CME) both have the ability to render our 21st century civilization null and void, pushing us back into the non-electronic 19th century.  Imagine no electricity, no Internet, no TV, no phones, no fuel for your car (if it will even run), and no factories running.

While most Hazard Planning resources share certain commonalities, catastrophic incidents (natural, manmade, or otherwise) may have cascading effects that exceed the boundaries of traditional emergency planning. It is therefore the explicit intent of this monograph to serve as a guide and resource to familiarize planners with current best practices associated with surviving a possible EMP event.

If the grid goes down, it is important to have prepared before the EMP/CME event.  People who live along the Gulf Coast have prepared for hurricanes for decades.  This planning process is very similar, but more detailed.  In the following, there are shorter timeframes noted. However, for all practical purposes, the longer timeframe, i.e., 4 to 12 months and beyond, should be the path chosen.  Shorter timeframes can be used when the effects of an EMP or CME event are not widespread, but this would be unlikely. They are shown here for comparative purposes. It is also important to recognize this is not a "one size fits all" approach.  Some of these ideas may work while others may not.  You must decide what works best depending on your needs and resources.

There may be some items that are not applicable to your situation. That is OK. You may need items not listed here. That, too, is OK. This is a planning tool, hopefully getting you to think about your situation and providing tools to help you and your family survive until recovery from an EMP or CME event is possible, which may be awhile.  Everyone's situation is different.

Note also that this is an overview. Books have been written on each planning element in more detail than presented here.

# Electromagnetic Pulse (EMP)

An EMP is defined as an intense burst of electromagnetic energy caused by an abrupt rapid acceleration of charged particles, most notably electrons. This rapid burst of energy is capable of causing severe damage to electronic equipment and devices, and may even result in physical damage to buildings, airplanes and power lines. Examples of EMPs: Lightning, nuclear explosion, and solar storm geomagnetic disturbances.

Nuclear Explosion (High altitude detonation of an EMP Type Weapon): All nuclear explosions produce EMP. A weapon can be enhanced to optimize EMP at high altitude, but even the tower-mounted Trinity test in 1945 produced a lot of EMP damage. Many people seem to think that EMP is a new type of weapon when the nuclear EMP effect has actually been observed for 70 years.

High-altitude EMP is produced in the stratosphere between 20km and 40km above the earth's surface. The air in the ionosphere is too thin to produce any significant EMP, and the widely spaced free electrons are too small to have much of an interaction with the gamma radiation. To produce EMP, one factor necessary is the electrons are accelerated to a very high speed (relativistic velocities).

In the stratosphere, however, conditions are just right for this. Gamma rays hit atoms of nitrogen or oxygen and eject the electrons at enormous speeds. The rest of the atom that is positively charged is much heavier, and so receives very little acceleration. The air is thick enough to insure most of the gamma rays collide with an atom, and yet thin enough to allow the ejected electrons to travel for a significant distance in the stratosphere. The gamma radiation does the ionization. The air does not have to be pre-ionized. In fact, pre-ionized air forms a bit of an electromagnetic shield.

The electrons ejected by gamma radiation would travel in a downward surge in the absence of a planetary magnetic field. In the presence of the Earth's magnetic field, however, the electrons are immediately deflected at a right angle, and begin to spiral around the Earth's magnetic field lines.

This interaction with the geomagnetic field causes the resulting EMP to be more than 1,000 times as strong as it would if the electrons just traveled linearly downward. This effect is also one of the reasons why the EMP from the Starfish Prime detonation caused relatively little damage in Hawaii. In tropical regions, the Earth's magnetic field is much weaker than it is in higher latitudes. Starfish Prime would have been much more intense over the continental United States.

Incidentally, in near-surface nuclear explosions, electrons traveling in a straight line produce the EMP, because the electrons hit air molecules in the dense air before they have time to interact with the Earth's magnetic field. So near-surface nuclear EMP fields fall off quickly with distance from the burst. However, the strong fields near the burst couple very large currents to long lines that run through or near ground zero. These currents are strong enough to affect systems tens of kilometers away. This was a problem in early nuclear tests only because they had control and telemetry wires that were running all the way in to the detonation point.

EMP is radiated out to the horizon of the burst location, affecting a circular area of the Earth's surface with a radius that can extend to thousands of kilometers. Because of the downward tilt of Earth's magnetic field over the U.S., the maximum EMP occurs south of the detonation and the minimum occurs to the north.

The resulting massive electrical surges would severely damage all types of electrical and electronic equipment (e.g., transformers, power grids, Supervisory Control and Data Acquisition (SCADA) plant control systems, computers, electronics) and virtually anything dependent on electricity.

Previous well-documented CME/EMP events include:

- **Carrington Event of 1859:** The first documented Solar Flare, named after solar astronomer Richard Carrington.

- **Star Fish Prime Test (U.S. 1962):** A 1.4 megaton nuclear warhead was detonated 250 miles into the atmosphere and over the Pacific Ocean (Hawaii, 900 miles away, experienced damaged street lights and microwave links).

Americans have become increasingly dependent on electronic technology and the electric power grid. As a result of this technological dependence, a major EMP/CME event can be considered a "civilization ending" occurrence. Based on a previous U.S. study, it is estimated that a major EMP incident will result in deaths of up to 90 percent of the American population within one year.

There are three EMP types: E1, E2 and E3.

- E1 is referred to as the EMP "fast pulse." It has a very brief duration, lasting less than a microsecond, but is extremely intense. Example: a Nuclear Blast or other EMP weapon. E1 is a very brief but intense electromagnetic field that induces extremely high voltages in electrical conductors. E1 causes most of its damage by causing electrical breakdown voltages to be exceeded. E1 can destroy computers and communications equipment and it changes too quickly for ordinary surge protectors to provide effective protection against it, although there are special fast-acting surge protectors that will block the E1 pulse.

- E2 is referred to as the EMP "intermediate pulse." Its duration is longer than E1, lasting several milliseconds. E2 has many similarities to lightning, although lightning-induced E2 may be considerably larger than a nuclear E2. Because of the similarities and the widespread use of lightning protection technology, E2 is generally considered to be the easiest to protect against.

- E3 is referred to as the EMP "slow pulse." It is caused by the nuclear detonation's temporary distortion of the Earth's magnetic field. The slowest of all pulses, it may last for minutes, hours, or even days. The E3 pulse is very similar to the pulses produced by geomagnetic storms. Like a geomagnetic storm, E3 can induce currents in long electrical conductors, damaging components such as power line transformers.

# Event Horizon Timelines

*Immediate:*    1st week

*Short-term:*    1 week – 1 month

*Medium-term*:    1 – 3 months

*Long-term:*    4 – 12 months and beyond

# Critical Planning Elements

- ☐ Books/Knowledge
- ☐ Water
- ☐ Food
- ☐ Clothing
- ☐ Sanitation
- ☐ Shelter
- ☐ First Aid/Medical
- ☐ Communications
- ☐ Alternative Power Sources
- ☐ Transportation
  - Individual Survival Equipment / "Bug Out Bag"
  - Vehicle Kits
- ☐ Miscellaneous

Operational Security (OpSec) is vital during survival preparation for an EMP/CME event. It is important dealing with limited resources in each Critical Planning Element to maintain OpSec because allowing people to know what you have could jeopardize your security and even survival.

Let's take each category and examine the elements for the different event horizons.

## Books/Knowledge

One of the most important things a person can do to prepare for the possibility of living after an EMP/CME event is to imagine what life might be like in those conditions. There have been numerous books, both fiction and nonfiction, and a number of films produced in recent years that portray a "grid down" America.

The international insurance giant Lloyds of London recently conducted a study into the economic damages associated with a hypothetical loss of the Northeastern U.S. Grid due to cyber-attack:

> Emerging Risk Report 2015 – Business Blackout[9]

A.M. Best, a leader in the insurance industry, published a paper in July 2015 on insuring the grid:

> Insuring the Grid: Damage to the Power Infrastructure Could Send a Shock to Insurers[10]

There are a few books that have been widely recognized as a "must read" on this topic. Three are listed below:

- *One Second After* by William R. Forstchen
- *EMP: Equipping Modern Patriots* by Jonathan Hollerman
- *Lights Out* by David Crawford

---

[9]   http://www.lloyds.com/~/media/files/news   and   insight/risk   insight/2015/business blackout/business blackout20150708.pdf

[10]   http://www.thefreelibrary.com/Insuring+the+grid%3A+damage+to+the+power+infrastructure +could+send+a...-a0421769187

Another aspect of "Knowledge" and in the area of reading is on the subject of living without electricity. In a "grid down" America, books on the skills and applications of the most recent pre-electric society will be essential. The need for this knowledge in establishing a society without electricity is critical. These skills can also be used for bartering.

Useful books related to an EMP or CME event include:

- *The Foxfire Book Series*[11]

- *The Forgotten Skills of Self-Sufficiency Used By the Mormon Pioneers*[12]

- *Wildwood Wisdom*[13]

- *Back to Basics: A Complete Guide to Traditional Skills, Third Edition*[14]

- *Back to Basics: A complete Guide to Traditional Skills* (Hardcover)[15]

- *Boy Scout Handbook*[16]

- *The Ultimate Encyclopedia of Knots & Ropework,*[17] Geoffrey Budworth

- *Field & Stream, The Total Outdoorsman Manual,*[18] T. Edward Nickens

- *The Comprehensive Guide to Tracking,* Cleve Cheney[19]

- *The Trapper's Bible,* Dale Martin[20]

Many of these are available in PDF format. The internet is an excellent source of information. These documents, and many others such as medical texts, can be put onto one of the original Kindles, which can store up to

---

[11]   http://www.foxfire.org/thefoxfirebookseries.aspx
[12]   http://www.amazon.com/Forgotten-Skills-Self-Sufficiency-Mormon-Pioneers/dp/1599555107
[13]   http://www.shelterpub.com/building/wildwood-wisdom
[14]   http://www.amazon.com/Back-Basics-Complete-Traditional-Edition/dp/1602392331
[15]   http://www.peregrinebookcompany.com/book/9781629143699
[16]   http://www.scouting.org/scoutsource/HealthandSafety/GSS/toc.aspx
[17]   http://www.amazon.com/Ultimate-Encyclopedia-Knots-Ropework-Step/dp/1844768910
[18]   http://www.amazon.com/Total-Outdoorsman-Manual-Field-Stream/dp/1616280611
[19]   http://www.amazon.com/Comprehensive-Guide-Tracking-depth-information/dp/1571574271
[20]   http://www.amazon.com/Trappers-Bible-Traps-Snares-Pathguards/dp/0873644069

3,000 books. These can be charged by a small solar panel, giving you a repository of knowledge.


# Water

Aside from air, the most important resource to have in a survival situation is water.

A human being can go without food for as long as three weeks, under harsh environments this figure is less. Without water, however, a human cannot survive more than three days; less time in high heat. ***Water should be your highest priority for survival. Without water, you will not survive!***

You must find a way to secure water, whether it is from a pond, stream, river, well, lake, swimming pool (use caution for pools as they may contain unacceptable levels of chemicals for treatment) or other sources. *Storing large amounts of water is only a temporary respite: Eventually you will need a regular source of water*.

One immediate source people rarely think about is the hot water heater in their home. This can be accessed easily with a garden hose and can yield 20 to 200 gallons, depending on the size and number of hot water heaters.


## Needs

***Immediate:***
Adults need approximately 3 quarts per day just for consumption. For planning purposes, round this up to one gallon/person/day. Remember, even more water will be needed for cooking, cleaning and sanitary use. Bottled water should suffice for this time frame. Another way to provide water is to fill tubs or containers with water while it is available.

***Short-Term:***
For those who live where there is adequate rainfall, some type of catch collection system should be considered, e.g., runoff from gutters into collection barrels. At this point the issue of purification comes into play.

Filters such as Big Berkey filters (2 filters are good for 6,000 gallons) are excellent for this task. Smaller Berkey "sport bottles" can also be used on an individual basis.

You can also make your own filtration system using the filters available for a Big Berkey and 5-gallon pails available from hardware stores. Berkey is not the only manufacturer; others also make good equipment. Katadyn and Sawyer offer a variety of water purification options that would allow you to survive by drinking from mud puddles for a long time. Popular brand water filters such as Brita and Zero Water are also great options.

Perhaps one of the most affordable and internationally renowned brands of water purification systems is from LifeStraw by the Vestergaard brand. The individual LifeStraw (approximately $20) is extremely lightweight and can be stored in one's "go bag" or vehicle at all times and can filter 1,000 liters (264 gallons) of water. The LifeStraw 1.0 is another very portable and relatively inexpensive ($75) option that will purify water for groups of people (up to 18,000 liters or 4,755 gallons).

***This equipment must be obtained <u>before</u> an event — it will not be available after an event.***

You can purchase food-grade plastic drums designed for water storage if you have space and budget. These typically hold 55 gallons of water; and with the addition of proper purification chemicals water will stay safe for up to five years. *This is not a long-term solution.*

Chlorine dioxide is a commonly occurring chemical and is used in many brands of water purification tablets and can be purchased relatively cheaply. Bleach (unscented) is probably the cheapest way to purify water. Strain cloudy water first through a bandana or other cloth for better results, mix ¼ teaspoon into 1 gallon of water, shake and let sit one hour. For less than $1.00 per gallon, 20 gallons of bleach from your local dollar store will yield approximately 42 years (RIGHT, 42 YEARS!) worth of purified water for a family of four (assuming you have access to a water source).

Boiling water for about 4-7 minutes will also purify water and distillation will purify both fresh and saltwater. Two 2-liter bottles, plastic tubing and a roll of black electrical tape and sunshine is all you need for a water still. If a water source is not an option you can dig a 2 X 2 foot hole in the ground; fill it halfway with grass, leaves or any plant material containing water; place a bowl in the center; cover it with clear plastic sheeting with a rock in the center above your bowl; and the sun will cause the water in the plant material to evaporate onto the plastic and drip into your bowl. A container of salt water instead of plant material will yield the same result. Lining the hole first with a Mylar survival blanket will greatly increase the evaporation rate for this system. However, this is not a long-term solution and will not work well in extremely arid climates.[21]

If you have a family of five (assume all adults) and your needs are a gallon per day per person (consumption only), this is only 450 gallons of water (90 days x 1 gallon/day x 5 people). This could be easily stored in eight 55-gallon drums (rounded). Storage could be in a garage or a basement and would not take up much room.

If you live in a subdivision or are on municipal water, it will stop very quickly as the pumps shut down from loss of power. You do not want to be looking for water a week into a disaster like a grid down situation without prior planning. Your survival hangs in the balance.

Wells, if available, are an excellent water source, as long as you have power to run the pump. Beyond the regular utilities are generators, solar panels, and manual pumps. Some solar pumps and manual pumps have depth limitations, so plan ahead with these tools:

- Deep Well Double-Acting Force Pump[22]

- Stainless Steel Pump[23]

An alternative for wells shallower (to the static water level) than about 50 feet is to install a hand pump. For static water levels of 23 to 50 feet, you still have to remove the submersible pump. Replace it with a hand lever connected to a rod that goes down the well to actuate a submersible piston pump. This is a moderate cost but involves some work. If you have a well

---

21  http://thesurvivalmom.com/wp-content/uploads/2010/08/Comprehensive-Preparedness-Manual.pdf

22  https://www.lehmans.com/p-4794-deep-well-double-acting-force-pump.aspx

23  http://www.survivalunlimited.com/waterpumps/sppricelist.htm

dedicated to the use of a hand pump, you can pay a professional to do all this work before the onset of an emergency.[24]

Another useful device if you have a well but no power for the pump is a length of PVC (or galvanized metal) that is open on one end with a ball valve on the other end called a well bucket.

It can be secured by a rope/chain at the top and lowered into the well by hand. Several such devices include:

- Lehman's Own Galvanized Well Bucket[25]
- DIY Water Well Bucket With Pictures[26]
- Emergency Well Tube[27]

Generators will be useful _as long as you have a fuel supply_ (assuming they are still functional), so planning beyond the eventuality of running out of fuel is necessary. If you decide to use solar power, you will need to obtain a solar pump capable of being powered by a solar panel (see solar pump depth limitations on page 20). Typically, a solar panel array; a solar charge controller; a battery system to power the pump; and the solar panel/battery capable of powering the pump will be needed. This will be covered in more detail under **Alternative Power Sources**.

Having spare solar panels and spare charge controllers is a good idea. An inverter should also be considered as part of a solar system. In most cases, it will not be necessary to run the pump for extended periods of time, only long enough to supply current needs, which could be running the pump for as little as 30 minutes per day. **_This equipment must be obtained before an event — it will not be available after an event._**

Medium-term to long-term will have the same **Needs** as the short-term periods. The difference is in the amount of resources required.

If your static water level is less than 23 feet deep, removing your nonfunctional electric submersible pump is not necessary. Instead, install a

---

24   EarthStraw "Code Red" 100 Foot Hand Well Pump System,
http://www.amazon.com/EarthStraw-Code-Foot-Hand-System/dp/B00O314QZW
25   https://www.lehmans.com/p-1384-lehmans-own-galvanized-well-bucket.aspx
26   http://americanpreppersnetwork.net/viewtopic.php?f=125&t=36709
27   http://emergencywelltube.com/order-mail/

pitcher pump at the top. It sucks water up through the unpowered submersible pump. You can install it yourself at moderate cost or you can pay a professional to do it for you. Being able to install an emergency system ahead of time is a real advantage over trying to do it after the onset of disaster.[28]

## Food

### *Immediate:*

Unfortunately, most people do not have the means to stay in their homes with the food they have in their pantry for more than 3-5 days. Immediate food needs can be satisfied with various canned and dried goods. In an emergency without power, it would be prudent to use the foods in the refrigerator and freezer first, before they spoil, then move on to the canned and dried foods. Start with foods that do not need heated or cooked in order to conserve fuel. Keep in mind you may need to have some way of heating or cooking the food in the freezer.

If you find yourself on the road trying to get home (i.e., you're at the office or away from your house) at the time of an event, a "Bug Out Bag" (BOB) would be useful getting home. It can contain energy bars; trail mixes; freeze dried food pouches of various types; staples such as tuna in foil packs; and various other helpful items, such as minor first aid, extra socks, maps, a knife, water bottles, a Berkey Sport Filter, etc. The **Transportation** section covers more information about "Bug Out Bags" (BOBs).

### *Short-Term:*

When stockpiling food for your family, choose food items familiar to them that require little to no heating. Cooking requires substantially more fuel than heating; therefore, canned foods that only need heated are a better choice than dried foods that require boiling. Oversize cans are great if you think your family can consume all the contents in one sitting, otherwise the leftovers will spoil in the absence of refrigeration. And, in a grid down scenario, you should try not have any waste of critical food items.

---

[28] http://www.empblog.org/tag/pitcher-pump/

When considering what to stock, peanut butter (assuming no allergies) and beans are great sources of protein and last for a long time. ***Make sure you have at least two mechanical can openers.*** Electric openers will not work. Remember: Two is one, one is none.

One method of stockpiling a short-term food supply is to use 5-gallon buckets to store a variety of canned foods (canned meats, veggies, pastas, etc. for a quantity of balanced meals). Include a small mechanical can opener; tape an index card on the top of the bucket with the quantities and types of canned foods along with the expiration date of the earliest expiring item.

You can calculate the number of days' worth of food each bucket contains for your family so you can quickly determine how much time you have with the numbers of buckets. As food is consumed the buckets can be used as a method of gathering and transporting water, etc. As the buckets approach the food expiration date you can either consume the food or donate it to your church, local charity, or food pantry. Note: When you fill these buckets, ensure the canned food is the same temperature as the surrounding air to eliminate condensation on the metal cans that could cause them to rust while in storage.

### Medium-term to Long-term:
This timeframe will have the same needs as the short-term period, just different amounts of resources. An excellent food calculator is provided online by the Latter Day Saints (LDS). [29] Their philosophy requires a year's supply of food for each family member. Another food storage calculator is available from the Food Guys. [30]

An Excel spreadsheet from Food Storage Made Easy can be used to calculate food requirements.[31] It also has a timeframe feature.

These charts are excellent resources for survival planning in the aftermath of an EMP/CME event.

---

[29]  http://lds.about.com/library/bl/faq/blcalculator.htm
[30]  http://www.thefoodguys.com/foodcalc.html
[31]  http://foodstoragemadeeasy.net/2009/03/09/long-term-food-storage-calculator/

Other thoughts on food for a forward planning process are to use food dehydrators, vacuum packing, pressure or hot water canning (much like our forefathers used) and freeze-drying. Food can also be stored in 5 gallon pails, using Mylar bags and oxygen absorbers, for as long as 25 years. Foods amenable to storing this way include beans, oats, and other grains such as red and white wheat, sugar, salt, rice, flour and pastas. An online search will show vendors of equipment and techniques for this method. Bulk packages of the above can be found at stores like Sam's, Costco, Walmart, and your local grocery store.

Dehydrators can dehydrate food for storage in Mason jars and food stored like this can last for long periods. Vacuum packing can be done with a vacuum sealer. You can vacuum seal just about anything for long-term storage. A vacuum sealer can also be used to vacuum seal Mason jars. Pressure canning uses a pressure vessel and boiling water. Foods so prepared can last for several years, properly stored. Storage should be in as cool and dark a place as is available, in any case, not exposed to sun and high heat. After a year, they may lose some quality, but will remain safe to eat as long as the seal is intact and the top is not bulging. If you live in a relatively cool climate, a root cellar can be used for food storage since it maintains a cool temperature throughout the year.

Freeze drying is possible at home. However, the basic investment is not cheap, typically around $3,000-$4,000.

It is also possible to seal #10 cans at home and then nitrogen purge them before sealing. A typical mechanical can sealer is around $950+, plus the nitrogen equipment.

There are many vendors who sell freeze-dried foods, vacuum-sealed foods and Meals Ready to Eat (MRE's). Some vendors are Mountain House, Augason Farms, Wise Foods, Numanna, Provident Pantry and others.

A grain mill is a necessity for storing grains. This will allow you to mill it to produce flour. Mechanical and electric mills are available, but the electric mills will only work if you have power from a solar panel or generator, so try to get a mechanical mill.

Natural honey is another item to consider. It stores well and is an excellent sweetener. It also has medicinal uses. Nuts (pistachios, cashews, pecans, peanuts and brazil nuts are all packed with protein and a variety of vitamins and minerals needed to sustain proper nutrition) and peanut butter are also long-term food storage items you should consider and will last almost indefinitely if stored properly.

Many communities have a local LDS food distribution center that will usually sell to non-LDS members. They are more limited than online vendors in selection, but cheaper and do not have shipping costs associated with them. There are also small stoves available which use a minimal amount of fuel. However, a better choice is a solar oven. It uses sunlight and will cook bread, chicken or boil water. They are frequently used in undeveloped countries. You can buy or build one.[32]

Finally, there is the organic, or gardening approach. Many people have enough land to put in a small garden. It is surprising how much a small garden can produce for a family. Obviously, this is not a last minute approach. You will need to decide what to grow and where, and make a decision when to start. It can take weeks or months to get produce from your garden. Heirloom seeds are a must. Hybrid seeds will not germinate for successive growing seasons like heirloom seeds.

Check out the resources below for heirloom seeds:

- Heirloom Seeds[33]
- Johnny's Selected Seeds[34]

Growing gardens in traditional rows will attract unwanted attention so planting stealth or circular gardens based around a fruit or nut tree with bushy plants and herbs next and ground vines or low growing plants next can yield a great amount of food and most people will not recognize this as a garden. Using perennials for this method will also yield food year after year without the need for replanting. Medicinal herbs can also be included which can aid in protecting your food plants from insects as well.

---

[32] http://www.instructables.com/id/Best-Solar-Oven/
http://www.motherearthnews.com/diy/how-to-build-solar-oven-zmaz74zhol.aspx
[33] http://heirloomseeds.com/
[34] http://www.johnnyseeds.com/

The one major issue here is water. If you live in an area with adequate rainfall, you should do well without having to water your garden. In an arid area, water may be more precious to drink rather than to use for watering. An excellent book on this topic is *Mini Farming: Self Sufficiency on ¼ Acre* by Brett Markham. There are many other equally good books on this subject. Plan ahead!

Stockpiling paper plates and plastic utensils minimizes or even eliminates the need to use water to wash dishes, utensils or serving items.

Hunting is another way to supplement food supplies. Many people, including your neighbors, may be occasional or avid hunters. If you decide to hunt, remember that other people may be doing the same. Depending on your locale, there may be a few or many other hunters competing for a limited amount of game. Learning to hunt with a bow is a capability that if practiced can be used to take any large to medium sized game. Blowguns are a great option for small game as are traps and snares. *The Trappers Bible* by Dale Martin is an excellent reference.

Fishing is another food source. If you are located by a stream, river, lake or larger body of water it will almost certainly have aquatic animals you can harvest. The type and abundance depends on your geographic location and could range from oysters or clams to crawfish, crabs, shrimp, turtles and fish. An ample supply of fishing line and a variety of different size hooks should be an essential part of your food supply planning. Trot lines, crab traps, minnow traps, seine nets and cast nets can be invaluable tools for harvesting seafood. Learning to construct fish traps from natural materials should also be part of your food supply plans.

## Clothing

There are really two basic levels for clothing: Immediate and all other. For immediate, you will typically have what you need already at home. The amount of each item will depend on your existing resources and how much extra you want to stock. When putting together a "Bug Out Bag", extra socks are a necessity, no matter where you live. In warm climate, good cover, e.g., a hat, would be useful, as well as good shoes/boots. Long sleeve shirts will provide protection from the sun and cold. A mosquito head net could be very useful in temperate climates and it is extremely compact and lightweight. Cold climates require warmer clothing to protect from the elements.

For longer periods, you may still have what you need at home, but consider that you may not be able to replace clothing items easily. Therefore, extra things such as underwear, socks, jeans, shirts, winter gear and rain gear should also be considered, as well as extra footwear. From a long-term/survival/tactical point of view, you cannot have too many socks and you need to keep your fingers protected. _Gloves should be high on the list._ Consider getting many pairs as they may be in use for a long time. You should get work gloves, gloves for cold weather and thinner calfskin gloves for tactical use.

Women should consider extra bras. With respect to children, remember, they grow so you may need to stock larger sizes, even though you may not need them right away. Towels and other bathing/hygiene items should also be on the list. Below is a list of items to consider maintaining at your home for short-term needs (climate dependent):

- 1 pair hiking/combat boots, preferably broken-in
- 6 pair hiking socks (they are thicker than regular socks)
- 1 pair heavy wool socks (for colder climates)
- 2 sets T-shirts for under layer in hot weather
- 2 pair cargo pants/shirts
- Heavy belt for holsters (guns)
- Hats — baseball/boonie/fleece beanie
- Gore-Tex rainwear/parka/pants
- Polartec medium weight jacket
- Mylar survival blanket

Items to consider purchasing (resources dependent) for long-term needs (climate dependent) should include the aforementioned items, _but in a double quantity_: Two is one, one is none. Also, you may want to add a Balaclava, a jumpsuit for hunting and a headscarf.

Purchasing these quantities of clothing for a "just in case" scenario could be expensive so consider shopping at a place like Goodwill or bargain outfitters where you can get discounted prices.

# Sanitation

The importance of personal hygiene during a crisis cannot be overemphasized. Sanitation is critical for several reasons. Accumulating waste, e.g., boxes, trash, etc., tells others someone lives here and could make you a target. Trash and bathroom wastes are important because you do not want to contaminate any water supplies, nor create a potentially hazardous medical situation due to attracting flies or providing a breeding ground for bacteria.

### *Immediate:*
Considerations should be given to extra toilet paper (which will become a true commodity for the long term!); wipes; porta potties made using 5-gallon buckets and trash liners; and somewhere to dump the waste. Latex/nitrile gloves can also be used to great effect when conducting cleaning/sanitation of waste areas, etc. Keep in mind some people are allergic to latex, therefore nitrile may be preferable.

If you have available water, you can fill the bowl of your toilet, but flushing may be an unwise use of a critical resource. Additionally, your community sewer system probably won't work. A septic system or treatment plant (still needs power, but solar can work) is preferable in this situation, but you may still need water to flush.

Antibacterial wipes and some type of hand sanitizer are also necessities. What may have been a minor cut could now be life threatening. This will be covered further under **First Aid/Medical.**

### *Short-term / Medium-term to Long-term:*
Needs here are similar to the Immediate needs, but quantities of resources are greater. No matter how much toilet paper you stock, you will eventually run out. What do you use? Spare pieces of cloth work well and

can be washed if you have enough water. Plant leaves also work, as long as you don't use something like poison ivy.

A shovel should be added to your supplies since you may need to bury waste. A good supply of plastic trash bags is also recommended for waste disposal.

Bleach is necessary for disinfecting.

Feminine products should also be obtained. Quantities should be based on the number of people needing these products.

## Shelter

### Immediate:
Neither an EMP event nor a CME will have any physical effect on a human body. Therefore, the question becomes: How do you want to shelter for the duration of whatever happens? In the immediate timeframe, getting to your home base is a priority, as that is probably where you have most of your supplies stored.

### Short-term:
In the short-term, it is important to make decisions about the viability of your facility. Is it in a safe location, i.e., safe from those who may not have planned well and are looking for resources (and who may be violent and have large numbers)? Can it be easily defended? Is it located near a water supply? Can the windows be opened for cooling (as opposed to a high rise apartment with windows that cannot be opened)? Are there adequate areas to store resources?

Mosquito nets are an important purchase in order to keep out bugs if you need to open windows for cooling your living space; as are tarps to create outdoor covered spaces for cooking and other activities that would have otherwise taken place indoors. Adding several hundred feet of 550 Para Cord (a 1,000 ft. roll can be purchased for less than $50 at Cheaper

Than Dirt[35]) is also an invaluable supply asset and can be used for many applications, from building shelters to animal snares and fishing line.

### Medium-term to Long-term:
In this timeframe, expect to stay where you are for the foreseeable future. Without the grid and power, you will not be as mobile as you previously were. All of the comments for short-term situations will apply, in addition to others. Will you have any close family members who will move in with you? If so, do you have enough room? Years ago, large families living in one home was normal. Do you have something to board up windows if necessary? Do you have a good relationship with your neighbors? You may need their help. Depending on the seasons, can you withstand a cold winter or warm summer in your present home?

Many individuals have a "bugout" location. The thought here is the location will provide shelter, be off the grid, and away from potential crowds/predators. If the grid goes down, how will you get to such a location? Your vehicle may operate, but fuel will be scarce, if even available, so you may only get as far as one tank of gas will carry you. In addition, if you have transportation and others do not, you become a target (more on this under **Transportation**).

Many people try to locate their "bugout" locations far away from their current location. If resources are stored at that location, how secure is it? Can someone steal your resources; move into it; prevent you from securing it; or do you have someone taking care of it?


# First Aid/Medical

### Immediate:
Immediate medicine might consist of a supply of Aspirin or Ibuprofen and some Imodium. A small supply of hydrogen peroxide (note: this loses strength over time); a triple antibiotic ointment; iodine; and, Band-Aids would complete the immediate needs of a non-trauma first aid kit. Another item for consideration would be moleskin for blisters or blister specific

---

[35]   https://www.cheaperthandirt.net/?code=DOTNET

Band-Aids. In a grid-down situation you may find yourself walking more, and taking care of your feet is a critical issue.

Military style Individual First Aid Kits (IFAK) and trauma kits provide another component of medical readiness. Kits like this can be purchased from many sources:

- Fully Stocked Tactical Trauma Kit First Aid Bag[36]
- Rescue Essentials[37]
- EMT Trauma Kits[38]
- Elite First Aid Military IFAK Individual First Aid Kit[39]
- Individual First Aid Kit (IFAK)[40]

You might already have some items in these kits; purchasing one or more is highly recommended, as redundancy is a valuable commodity. Taking a first aid class, at a minimum, preferably an advanced class or a First Responder class is another preparatory measure.

### Short-term:
A larger supply of the medications listed above, as well as some antibiotics (since access to doctors might be difficult) should be considered. It's important to start off by noting that you will not want to indiscriminately use antibiotics for every minor ailment that comes along. You will want to wisely dispense that limited and precious supply of life-saving drugs.

You should have several good medical books on hand to help you diagnose the problem including dosage guides. Dosages below are average for adults and not for children or nursing mothers. Only when you are certain that antibiotics will help, should you take them.

---

[36] http://www.amazon.com/Stocked-Tactical-Trauma-First-Aid/dp/B003IPJ3O8
[37] http://www.rescue-essentials.com/tactical-kits/
[38] http://www.grainger.com/category/emt-trauma-kits/emt-and-rescue-supplies/safety/ecatalog/N-od4
[39] http://www.amazon.com/Elite-First-Aid-IFAK-Individual/dp/B00ABAELZE
[40] http://www.chinookmed.com/cgi-bin/category/LE-IFAK

Antibiotics to consider include:[41]

***Amoxicillin*** *250mg/500mg* will handle most of the same types of bacteria as Cephalexin. It is also safe for pregnant women and children and has very few side effects. However, some people are very allergic to it.

***Ampicillin*** *250mg/500mg* is similar to penicillin but more effective against things like anthrax and less likely to cause an allergic reaction. It is also useful for respiratory tract infections, bacterial meningitis, urinary tract infections, gastrointestinal infections and many other things.

***Ciprofloxacin*** *250mg/500mg* is best for ailments like urinary tract infections, prostate infections, respiratory tract infections (such as bronchitis or pneumonia), bacterial diarrhea, anthrax, and diverticulitis or infectious colitis (when combined with Metronidazole). Children, pregnant women and nursing mothers should never use it.

***Cephalexin*** *250mg/ 500mg* is great for almost any type of respiratory infection (bronchitis, pneumonia, strep throat, etc.) and middle ear infections. It is safe for pregnant women and children and only has a few side effects.

***Metronidazole*** *250mg is u*sually used for getting rid of anaerobic bacteria, which is found in the intestine. It can treat diverticulitis or colitis if taken with Ciprofloxacin; and can also treat bacterial vaginosis, diabetic foot ulcer, joint or bone infections, lung or brain abscesses, meningitis, and a few other infections. Children, pregnant women and nursing mothers should not take this.

***Doxycycline*** *100mg* treats the same types of infections as Erythromycin. However, Erythromycin can be hard to find. This can also treat sinus infections, Typhus and Malaria. There are some side effects including kidney impairment and sensitive skin. Children, pregnant women and nursing mothers should not use this medication.

***Sulfamethoxazole*** *400mg/**Trimethoprim*** 80mg* (SMZ-TMP) treat most respiratory infections when used together, but they are mainly used for urinary tract infections. The best thing about SMZ-TMP is it can treat

---

41   http://urbansurvivalsite.com/the-9-best-survival-antibiotics/

Methicillin-resistant Staphylococcus aureus (MRSA), also known as resistant staph. This is a strain of bacteria that spreads easily and is resistant to most antibiotics.

*Azithromycin 250mg/ 500mg* treats respiratory infections and all sorts of conditions like Chlamydia, Lyme Disease, Pelvic Inflammatory Disease, Syphilis, Typhus, etc. Side effects include abdominal pain, nausea and diarrhea but that is rare. It's a great antibiotic to have because it treats so many different problems. The difficulty is that it's hard to find and can be a bit expensive.

*Clindamycin 150mg/300mg* is used to treat certain types of bacterial infections, including infections of the lungs, skin, blood, female reproductive organs, and internal organs. This drug is not recommended for nursing mothers or pregnant women in the first trimester.

Antibiotics such as clindamycin will not kill the viruses that cause colds, flu, and other infections. It is used along with other medications to treat anthrax (a serious infection that may be deliberately spread as part of a terror attack) and malaria (a serious infection that is spread by mosquitoes in certain parts of the world). Clindamycin is also sometimes used to treat ear infections and toxoplasmosis (an infection that may cause serious problems in people who do not have healthy immune systems or in unborn babies whose mothers are infected) when these conditions cannot be treated with other medications.

*Erythromycin* 250mg/500mg can treat most respiratory infections and middle ear infections. It's also good for Syphilis, Lyme Disease and Chlamydia. It has several potential side effects including abdominal pain, nausea, vomiting and diarrhea. It is safe for women and children.

If you don't want to get every one of these, you should at least get Ciprofloxacin, Metronidazole and Cephalexin. These three will cover 9 out of 10 infections you might get. As far as storage, it is best to keep them in a cool dark place. You don't have to, but it will extend shelf life. They should continue to be effective for years after the expiration date, with one exception: Tetracyclines (which includes doxycycline) because it can become toxic if they get too old. Amounts to get will vary, but consider you are planning for these being unobtainable for the foreseeable future.

There are various others you can choose, but the selections above will give you the opportunity to treat many illnesses and have enough variety so that even those with Penicillin allergies with have options. Cephalexin, although not in the same drug family, has been quoted as having a 10% cross-reactivity rate with Penicillin.

Liberal use of antibiotics is a poor strategy for a few reasons:

1.  Overuse can foster the spread of resistant bacteria.

2.  Potential allergic reactions may occur that could lead to anaphylactic shock.

Many people have allergies. Several things to consider are a supply of Benadryl and several EpiPens for all stages of planning. They may save a life in a severe allergic reaction.

In addition to antibiotics, a good supply of bandages, topical antibiotic creams and more Imodium should be obtained. Aspirin, Ibuprofen and Tylenol should also be stocked in large quantities. Add to the list betadine wipes; gauze and tape to use in bandaging; inflatable splints; Vaseline (good for burns and skin abrasions); and a dental repair kit for temporary repair of fillings.

Those individuals on Insulin need to consider that it sometimes needs to be refrigerated. If refrigeration is necessary and there is no power, an old technology called a Zeer pot may be used. This is simply two clay pots with water saturated sand in between and works by evaporative cooling.

Try getting a prescription medicine supply from your doctor for those medications specifically prescribed to you or anyone in your family. Cardiac and specialty medicines such as Insulin, Synthroid, etc., may be difficult to obtain in quantity. This should be discussed with your physician.

In the event your doctor will not prescribe medicines, consider products like Fish Mox, fish antibiotics manufactured in the same dosage and packaging as its USP counterparts. (The United States Pharmacopeia Convention issues an annual convention on drug information) They are said to be identical and do not require a prescription to obtain.

*Medium-term to Long-term:*
All planning considerations for the short-term apply plus the quantity required should be increased substantially. It would be prudent to acquire things like suture kits, sutures, scalpels, a stethoscope, a blood pressure cuff, a thermometer, and tourniquets. Other items to consider are Quickclot, Celox, Hyfin chest seals, needles to relieve tension pneumothorax (requires training to use), and oil of cloves (for toothache). Aluminum splints (come in a roll), a ring cutter (in the event trauma to the finger requires ring removal), and an obstetrics kit should be considered. A large quantity of bandages of various sizes should be stocked, as well as a large quantity of triple antibiotic creams. Bandages specific for burns (containing Vaseline or water gel) should also be in your supplies. You should also consider eyewashes and alcohol or betadine: What was once an annoying cut could be life threatening.

A good supply of Imodium will also be important. Dehydration from diarrhea can be deadly.

You are planning for an event that may last several years before society is stabilized.

Another item for the medical supplies is honey. It has been used for centuries to promote healing. The most common medical use of honey is to treat sore throats. In treating wounds, honey not only destroys bacterial infections, it creates a moist healing environment that allows skin cells to regrow naturally. It has an acidic pH that is inhospitable for bacteria. It also has an osmotic effect that kills by drawing out fluid from the bacteria. Studies have shown honey heals wounds better and faster, with a dramatic decrease in infection rates, especially in burn injuries.

It can be applied to cuts; scrapes; burns of any depth if medical help is not available; rashes; and any open skin injury after good wound cleaning.

# Communications

Communications is one of the most overlooked items in planning for an emergency event. In a crisis, the ability to coordinate with others, contact emergency personnel or find out what is going on around you and much further away, is very valuable. In an EMP or CME event, it is very likely that most communications will be down. This means no cellphones, no phone landlines, and no internet. Satellite phones will also likely be inoperative as EMP will take out the satellites they use. How will you communicate with family members, emergency personnel or see what is going on in the next town or state?

### Immediate:
Immediate communications may be absent.   Most people rely on cellphones, landlines or the internet to communicate.  During Hurricane Katrina in 2005, when normal cellphones were not operative, people realized they could text on a different carrier band and still communicate. Cellphones probably will not work after an EMP or CME event. So, what to do? Calling home will not be an option since landlines will also be out. And, neither will CB radios due to their short range, usually less than 10 miles. Likewise, 2-way radios may not work since most are dependent on a digital network or operate on limited power. And, even if you have planned well ahead of time, very few types of communications will work.

You need to have a plan worked out ahead of time with family members of where to meet after a disaster.  That way, you will not need to communicate with anyone: You will have already decided on a course of action.

### Short-term / Medium to Long-term:
Both timeframes are included here because it is unlikely anything will change in the short-term.  What options will be available to you? Unless they are connected to chargers in your house, CB radios *may* still work.

The transmission range of a CB varies greatly with the type antenna; atmosphere; channel; number of other transmissions taking place; terrain; and solar activity.  Most mobile-to-mobile transmissions will be between your location and up to 10 miles out.  Some periods may allow "skip" or "DX" to occur resulting in transmission over 100 miles and up to 1,000 miles or more! Power is restricted to 4-watts on AM and 12-watts on SSB without an external amplifier (linear amplifier).  A CB frequency chart is below:

# CB Frequency Chart

| CB Channel | Frequency Use | Notes |
|---|---|---|
| Channel 1 | 26.965 MHz | |
| Channel 2 | 26.975 MHz | |
| Channel 3 | 26.985 MHz | Prepper CB Network (AM) |
| Channel 4 | 27.005 MHz | Used by many 4X4 clubs/ The American Pepper's Network |
| Channel 5 | 27.015 MHz | |
| Channel 6 | 27.025 MHz | Many operators using illegal linears (amplifiers of illegal power) |
| Channel 7 | 27.035 MHz | |
| Channel 8 | 27.055 MHz | |
| Channel 9 | 27.065 MHz | Universal C.B. Emergency / REACT Channel |
| Channel 10 | 27.075 MHz | |
| Channel 11 | 27.085 MHz | Local calling channel |
| Channel 12 | 27.105 MHz | |
| Channel 13 | 27.115 MHz | Often used in some areas for marine, RV's, and campers |
| Channel 14 | 27.125 MHz | FCMA (Federal Motor Coach Assoc) |
| Channel 15 | 27.135 MHz | Used by truckers in CA |
| Channel 16 | 27.155 MHz | Used by many 4X4 clubs |
| Channel 17 | 27.165 MHz | Used by truckers on the east-west roads in CA |
| Channel 18 | 27.175 MHz | |
| Channel 19 | 27.185 MHz | Unofficial main "Trucker" channel |
| Channel 20 | 27.205 MHz | |
| Channel 21 | 27.215 MHz | Used by truckers for N/S routes in CA and some other areas |
| Channel 22 | 27.225 MHz | |
| Channel 23 | 27.255 MHz | |
| Channel 24 | 27.235 MHz | |
| Channel 25 | 27.245 MHz | |
| Channel 26 | 27.265 MHz | Used by truckers for N/S routes in CA and some other areas |
| Channel 27 | 27.275 MHz | |
| Channel 28 | 27.285 MHz | |
| Channel 29 | 27.295 MHz | |
| Channel 30 | 27.305 MHz | Channels 30 and up are often used for SSB |
| Channel 31 | 27.315 MHz | |
| Channel 32 | 27.325 MHz | |
| Channel 33 | 27.335 MHz | |
| Channel 34 | 27.345 MHz | |
| Channel 35 | 27.355 MHz | |
| Channel 36 | 27.365 MHz | Unofficial USB calling channel |
| Channel 37 | 27.375 MHz | Prepper 37 (USB) |
| Channel 38 | 27.385 MHz | Unofficial LSB calling channel |
| Channel 39 | 27.395 MHz | SSB |
| Channel 40 | 27.405 MHz | SSB |

Source: http://offgridsurvival.com/shtf-emergency-communications/

In addition, Family Radio Service (FRS) or General Mobile Radio Service (GMRS) *may* work. Many CB radios, FRS and GMRS radios work off batteries. They all have a relatively short range, 1-5 miles under ideal conditions. Although FRS and GMRS radios are advertised to have 25-mile ranges, this is unrealistic.

Also, if you live in an area with many trees, they will attenuate the signal. If your radios still work, this will give you communications with friends and neighbors in a small area. Additionally, you may want to consider stockpiling batteries or rechargeable batteries capable of being recharged by a small solar panel. This will provide a long-lasting source of power.

There are 22 FRS / GMRS channels. Channels 1–7 are shared with the GMRS. Channels 8–14 are for FRS only. Channels 15–22 are for GMRS only. It should be noted that the FRS does not require licensing where the GMRS requires a FCC license. The FRS radios are restricted to ½ watt (500-milliwatts) and must have a fixed antenna. The range of a typical FRS radio is typically ¼ mile out to approximately 1½ miles, sometimes further depending upon the terrain and other factors. GMRS radios may use up to 5-watts of power and offer better range. A list of frequencies for the FRS / GMRS is below:

### Frequencies for the FRS / GMRS

| Channel | Use | Frequency (MHz) | Channel | Use | Frequency (MHz) |
|---------|---------|-----------------|---------|------|-----------------|
| 1 | FRS/GMRS | 462.5625 | 12 | FRS | 467.6625 |
| 2 | FRS/GMRS | 462.5875 | 13 | FRS | 467.6875 |
| 3 | FRS/GMRS | 462.6125 | 14 | FRS | 467.7125 |
| 4 | FRS/GMRS | 462.6375 | 15 | GMRS | 462.5500 |
| 5 | FRS/GMRS | 462.6625 | 16 | GMRS | 462.5750 |
| 6 | FRS/GMRS | 462.6875 | 17 | GMRS | 462.6000 |
| 7 | FRS/GMRS | 462.7125 | 18 | GMRS | 462.6250 |
| 8 | FRS | 467.5625 | 19 | GMRS | 462.6500 |
| 9 | FRS | 467.5875 | 20 | GMRS | 462.6750 |
| 10 | FRS | 467.6125 | 21 | GMRS | 462.7000 |
| 11 | FRS | 467.6375 | 22 | GMRS | 462.7250 |

Moving up, we arrive at ham radios. Ham radios have been used during disasters such as hurricanes and major storms or earthquakes for decades. Again, will your radio work? And, if your radio works, who will you be able to talk to?

The articles below detail how ham radios have been used:

- Amateur Radio Plays Important Role in Boston Bombing[42]
- Ham Radio Operators to the Rescue After Katrina[43]
- Ham Radio Organization Aids Carrollton in Severe Weather situations[44]

There are several ways to improve the survivability of your radio. One, make sure it is not connected to the grid, i.e., plugged into a power supply or connected to an antenna. If so, it makes them vulnerable to an E1 or E3 pulse generated by EMP. You should consider disconnecting your radio from a home power supply and antenna when not in use.

Many ham operators choose to have a backup radio stored in an improvised Faraday cage. These are simple to construct out of a metal trashcan with a lid that can be secured. The inside should be lined with cardboard, as well as the bottom, so that no part of the radio touches metal when it is placed inside.

What type of radios should you consider? Although the FCC requires a license to operate a ham radio, in an EMP or CME event, it is extremely unlikely that anyone from the FCC will be looking for people without licenses. *It is still recommended to obtain a license.* In the process, you learn theory, as well as how to operate a radio, common language used in ham radio, call protocol, antenna design and capabilities of your radio.

The lowest level radio is a handheld UHF/VHF radio, or 2 Meter (2M)/70 Centimeter (70CM). The 2M frequency runs from 144.000 MHz to 148.000 MHz. The 70CM band runs from 420.00 to 450.00 MHz. These usually operate at 5 watts, a low power level that usually will not give you

---

[42] http://www.emergencymgmt.com/emergency-blogs/crisis-comm/Amateur-radio-plays-important-061813.html

[43] http://www.nbcnews.com/id/9228945/ns/technology_and_science-wireless/t/ham-radio-operators-rescue-after-katrina/#.VaPb-PlVhBc

[44] http://www.dallasnews.com/news/community-news/northwest-dallas-county/headlines/20150423-ham-radio-organization-aids-carrollton-in-severe-weather-situations.ece

much more range than the CB, FRS or GMRS radios. However, if you have a better antenna or go through a repeater, you may get better range. Keep in mind, you can only talk to someone who has a radio using the same radio bands. These radios are powered by batteries.

Next up is a mobile or base station 2M radio. Usually 2M is more common for everyday use than 70CM. These radios can be obtained in power levels up to 75 watts. It is also possible to buy amplifiers that boost this power considerably. Range on these radios with a good antenna can be up to 45 miles in simplex mode (point to point) without going through a repeater (a device that receives your signal and puts it out again, often at a higher power level in order to extend your range).

These radios are powered by a power supply that provides 13.8 volts. The power supplies are usually plugged into a wall outlet, so now there is another problem – no power! If your car is functioning, it is possible to run these radios off the car battery. But, eventually, that will run out. Let's cover the next level of ham radio and then address power.

Next, we arrive at the High Frequency, or HF, radio. These radios operate on completely different frequencies in specified bands of frequencies. They range in power from 5-20 watts (called a QRP radio) to 100 watts. Beyond the standard 100 watts, you can get amplifiers to increase the power, and thus, range. QRP radios and 100-watt radios can both communicate thousands of miles away under the right atmospheric conditions and with a good antenna. *To communicate in a circumference less than 400 miles, it may be necessary to use an NVIS (near vertical incidence skywave) antenna. If you go the ham radio route, it would be essential to have at least one such antenna available. This is a specialized antenna frequently used by the military and ham operators doing emergency work* (this information is available when studying for a ham license).

An antenna is the heart of a ham radio. You should consider having several antennas for a home station and possibly one or two portable antennas. For QRP radios, a good external tuner will allow the use of a random length of wire.

Most emergency communications are conducted on 2M, 40M (7000-7300 kHz) and 80M (3.5 to 4.0 MHz) and most ham operators know this.

## Amateur High-Frequency Emergency & Hurricane Nets

| Frequency Mode | Location |
|---|---|
| 03808.0 LSB | Caribbean Wx (Weather) |
| 03845.0 LSB | Gulf Coast West Hurricane |
| 03862.5 LSB | Mississippi Section Traffic |
| 03865.0 LSB | West Virginia Emergency |
| 03872.5 LSB | Mercury Amateur Radio Assoc/hurricane info net |
| 03873.0 LSB | West Gulf ARES Emergency (night) |
| 03873.0 LSB | Central Gulf Coast Hurricane, Louisiana ARES Emergency (night), Mississippi ARES Emergency |
| 03910.0 LSB | Central Texas Emergency, Mississippi ARES, Louisiana Traffic |
| 03915.0 LSB | South Carolina SSB NTS |
| 03923.0 LSB | Mississippi ARES, North Carolina ARES Emergency (Tarheel) |
| 03925.0 LSB | Central Gulf Coast Hurricane, Louisiana Emergency |
| 03927.0 LSB | North Carolina ARES (health & welfare) |
| 03935.0 LSB | Central Gulf Coast Hurricane, Louisiana ARES (health & welfare), Texas ARES (health & welfare), Mississippi ARES (health & welfare), & Alabama Emergency |
| 03940.0 LSB | Southern Florida Emergency |
| 03944.0 LSB | West Gulf Emergency |
| 03950.0 LSB | Hurricane Watch (Amateur-to-National Hurricane Center), Northern Florida Emergency |
| 03955.0 LSB | South Texas Emergency |
| 03960.0 LSB | North East Coast Hurricane |
| 03965.0 LSB | Alabama Emergency |
| 03967.0 LSB | Gulf Coast (outgoing traffic) |
| 03975.0 LSB | Georgia ARES, Texas RACES |
| 03993.5 LSB | Gulf Coast (health & welfare) |
| 03993.5 LSB | South Carolina ARES/RACES Emergency |
| 03995.0 LSB | Gulf Coast Wx |
| 07145.0 LSB | Bermuda |
| 07165.0 LSB | Antigua/Antilles Emergency and Weather, Inter-island 40-meter (continuous watch) |
| 07225.0 LSB | Central Gulf Coast Hurricane |
| 07232.0 LSB | North Carolina ARES Emergency |
| 07235.0 LSB | Louisiana Emergency, Central Gulf Coast Hurricane, Louisiana Emergency |
| 07240.0 LSB | American Red Cross US Gulf Coast Disaster, Texas Emergency |
| 07242.0 LSB | Southern Florida ARES Emergency |
| 07243.0 LSB | Alabama Emergency, South Carolina Emergency |
| 07245.0 LSB | Southern Louisiana |
| 07247.5 LSB | Northern Florida ARES Emergency |
| 07248.0 LSB | Texas RACES |
| 07250.0 LSB | Texas Emergency |
| 07254.0 LSB | Northern Florida Emergency |
| 07260.0 LSB | Gulf Coast West Hurricane |
| 07264.0 LSB | Gulf Coast (health & welfare) |

## Amateur High-Frequency Emergency & Hurricane Nets

| Frequency Mode | Location |
|---|---|
| 07265.0 LSB | Salvation Army Team Emergency Radio (SATERN) |
| 07268.0 LSB | Bermuda |
| 07273.0 LSB | Texas ARES |
| 07275.0 LSB | Georgia ARES |
| 07280.0 LSB | NTS Region 5, Louisiana Emergency |
| 07283.0 LSB | Gulf Coast (outgoing only) |
| 07285.0 LSB | West Gulf ARES Emergency (day), Louisiana ARES Emergency (day) |
| 07285.0 LSB | Mississippi ARES Emergency, Texas ARES Emergency (day) |
| 07290.0 LSB | Central Gulf Coast Hurricane, Gulf Coast Wx, Louisiana ARES (health & welfare day), Texas ARES (health & welfare), & Mississippi ARES |
| 14185.0 USB | Caribbean Emergency |
| 14222.0 USB | Health & Welfare |
| 14245.0 USB | Health & Welfare |
| 14265.0 USB | Salvation Army Team Emergency Radio (SATERN) (health & welfare) |
| 14268.0 USB | Amateur Radio Readiness Group |
| 14275.0 USB | Bermuda & International Amateur Radio |
| 14300.0 USB | Intercontinental Traffic & Maritime Mobile Service |
| 14303.0 USB | International Assistance & Traffic |
| 14313.0 USB | Intercontinental Traffic & Maritime Mobile Service |
| 14316.0 USB | Health & Welfare |
| 14320.0 USB | Health & Welfare |
| 14325.0 USB | Hurricane Watch (Amateur-to-National Hurricane Center) |
| 14340.0 USB | Louisiana (1900) |
| 21310.0 USB | Health & Welfare (Spanish) |
| 28450.0 USB | Health & Welfare (Spanish) |

Source: http://www.hurricane.alabama.gov/ham.htm

QRP radios can easily be operated by battery power or small solar panels. An HF radio consumes more power and will not operate for as long on battery power, but it can be done with larger solar panels and larger batteries. Solar panels may be your only source of power in a disaster.

By using ham radios, you may be able to communicate with whatever emergency departments are operating; friends across town or people farther away to find out what their status is.

# Alternative Power Sources

*Immediate:*
In the immediate timeframe, there are few choices. You may have battery power; and possibly a small solar charger for your electronics and the power in your automobile, if it is still running; and maybe a generator. Chances are, your home will be without power unless you have planned ahead.

*Short-term / Medium-term to Long-term:*
The first thing people fall back on is a portable or whole house generator. Portable electric generators are usually powered by diesel fuel, gasoline or propane. They are generally not adequate for powering an entire house and due to fuel conservation, this would not be recommended. They may, however, be very useful for powering critical items such as electric heaters, fans, and small pumps.

Gasoline is usually not the best fuel for a generator. The reasons are its short lifetime in storage, and the fact it is very flammable. If gasoline is all you have, consider a long-term fuel stabilizer. Even then, it will not last long.

Diesel fuel is less dangerous to have in storage from the viewpoint of flammability. It will also last in storage for two or three years if you add the proper diesel fuel preservative.

Portable generators converted to run on propane are also commonly available and most small engine shops can do this conversion. Propane will last much longer than other fuels used in portable generators, but even stored propane will not last forever. And, you will eventually run out of gasoline, diesel or propane.

The important thing to remember about a portable generator is that it will only supply standby power for a short time. An exception may be if you live in a rural area (i.e., a farm) with a large capacity fuel tank, preferably diesel. Even then, portable generators are not designed for continuous use during long-term power outages. You would want to run it for only a short time each day to pump a well or cool supplies and by doing so, conserve fuel.

The most popular whole-house generators in recent years are those that run on natural gas or propane. Natural gas generators have the advantage that many people have natural gas piped into their house already, so they don't have to worry about a fuel supply for ordinary power outages. Large-scale disasters, which include any scenario where a large part of the power grid is down for days or weeks, may not provide adequate gas flow to run such a generator. Hurricane Katrina is a good example where many areas had their supply of natural gas disrupted.

Many whole-house generators can be set up to run on propane. Propane tanks can be had in sizes of 250 gallons, 500 gallons, and 1,000 gallons and are usually filled to 80% of their nameplate capacity.

During any sort of a long-term power outage, most of the portable home generators (unlike industrial standby generators) must be shut down once a day or so for brief maintenance for things like checking the oil level. Other than these brief maintenance periods, the run time is generally limited only by the fuel supply.

*Much of the following material (and material in the Introduction) is used with kind permission by Jerry Emanuelson at http://futurescience.com, and we are grateful to him for his contribution. In addition, there is wealth of information on his website.*

Most manual-start portable generators should continue functioning **as long as no external wires are connected to them during the EMP event.** This means don't plug extension cords or other items into a portable generator until you actually need them. Leaving an unused portable generator with an extension cord plugged into it is just like connecting an EMP antenna to the interior. If you have a portable generator with obvious electronic "features," be sure you keep spare parts for the electronics, and keep the spare electronic parts in shielded containers.

For whole-house generators, have a voltage transient suppressor at the input (electric power grid side) of your transfer switch. If you don't have the time or money to search for and purchase a suppressor fast enough for EMP, at least have the electrician install a lightning protector on the input to your transfer switch.

Transtector and SOLA make voltage transient protectors that are supposed to be fast enough for nuclear EMP. These will only block the EMP coming in on the power line, but this is the most important part of the pulse. Voltage spikes coming in from the main power lines from EMP would range from many thousands to a million volts or more. In addition, if you live in a lightning-prone area, lightning-induced power line spikes are likely to destroy unprotected generator electronics sometime within the normal lifetime of your generator. There is also good transient protection built into the generator electronics, but that "good" transient protection is nearly always inadequate, even under normal conditions.

The excellent EMP power line transient suppressors by Transtector have gotten very expensive in recent years. Most Transtector transient suppressors are now more than a thousand dollars each. SOLA makes good transient protectors for half the price of the Transtector units. The SOLA model **STV 100K-10S** is an excellent unit made for the 120/240-volt systems that are the most common for U.S. residential use. It costs around $600 and will have to be wired in by an electrician.

There is also another lightning and transient suppressor that, according to its specifications, may be fast enough for shunting the incoming power line voltage spike from EMP. It is the Ditek HD2 for less than $300 and is available through many electrical distributors used by electrical contractors.

An EMP will induce much larger voltages on the power lines on the distant eastern and western horizons with respect to the detonation point. The eastern and western horizons may have voltages in excess of one million volts induced on long lines. The areas closer to the detonation point will be limited to induced voltages of something like 100,000 volts, even on the longest lines. Also, the transformer that feeds your home or building will slow down the rise time of the pulse on the power line so that even conventional transient suppressors will likely catch this part of the pulse. The greater danger comes from the fast-rise-time 50,000 to 100,000 volt pulse that is induced in the wiring close to and inside of your home or other building.

In addition to voltage transient protection for your generator, it is important to have transient protection for the critical and more sensitive electrical and electronic items in your house especially if you have a whole-house stationary generator. Every time your transfer switch switches the power either to the generator or back to the main power, it will create a voltage spike in your entire house.

Put at least an inexpensive consumer-type "surge suppressor" on every piece of important electrical device in your home. Inexpensive surge suppressors have gotten much better in the past few years, and every one you use will eventually pay for its cost. You won't realize that the surge suppressors are paying for themselves because you won't know about the electronics you would have been replacing due to premature failure.

Try to get an outlet surge protector that is rated for at least 3,000 joules, but any surge suppressor is better than nothing. Even the electrical outlets that you use for charging things like laptop computers and cell phones should have a surge suppressor.

Complete shielding of the electronics in a home generator system is rather difficult, but it is possible. It is usually a good idea to keep spare circuit boards and electronics modules on hand, if possible.

Unless specified as an "off-grid" or "island" system, most home solar PV (photo voltaic) systems — including rooftop solar power systems — are synchronized to the alternating current frequency of the power grid. This enables seamless import of utility power to the home at night and export of power from the solar panels during times of peak production. When failure of the power grid in the PV-equipped home's neighborhood occurs, protective systems in the solar power inverter shut down the home system for two reasons:

1. Prevent damage to the system inverter from massive overload when one home system attempts to power an entire neighborhood.

2. Eliminate the risk that power produced by the PV system will energize downed utility lines and expose repair crews to dangerous voltage.

Solar power systems commonly advertised on television are tied into the grid; they are not designed to power your home in an off grid situation. This is because they do not have a battery bank and an inverter to power your home. A battery bank adds cost and complexity to a system, but is the only way to power your home just on solar power. Such systems are not cheap, but also not prohibitively expensive.

EMP poses an additional danger to solar power systems since EMP can destroy all of the components of an unprotected solar power system. This includes solar panels, since the solar panels are just semiconductors that are open to the sky. Total EMP protection of a solar panel power system is possible, and needs not be terribly expensive. A qualified solar installer should be consulted.

In the event resources are not available to install a whole-house off-grid system, you can put together small solar panels with a charge controller and a battery (it is a good idea to have several batteries so one can be charging while the other is in use). This allows the battery to charge then use it to power small electronic appliances such as lights, fans, small refrigerators and radios.

This will be an absolute necessity for powering a small ham radio. Such systems are fairly inexpensive. A small Sealed Lead Acid (SLA) battery will work. But, due to their chemistry, they are inferior to the new breed of Lithium Iron Phosphate (LiFePO4) batteries. The LiFePO4 batteries are more expensive than their SLA counterparts, but can be charged up to 3,000 times; hold a charge for a very long time; but need special chargers. They also have a very different discharge curve. And, they are not dangerous and prone to fires like their Lithium Ion counterparts.

Shielded solar panels along with shielded and transient protected auxiliary solar equipment are the only real alternative that does not require ongoing fuel and frequent maintenance.

One of the newest recently announced technologies (not yet on the market) is the whole-house battery system called Powerwall by Tesla, which is charged by solar PV panels. Powerwall comes in 7 kWh and 10 kWh models. Both are guaranteed for 10 years and are sufficient to power most homes during peak evening hours. Multiple batteries, up to nine, may be installed together for homes with greater energy needs, up to 63 kWh total for the 7 kWh battery and 90 kWh total for the 10 kWh battery. Systems (not including the solar PV panels or inverters) run from $3,000 to $3,500. This is relatively new technology, but may be an excellent alternative power source.[45]

Obviously, it would have to be protected from transient surges, so this could incur additional cost.

There are other power sources, such as wood-fired boilers to provide steam, small water turbines and windmills, to name a few. While all are viable, each has its own unique issues, e.g., adequate firewood and water, moving water and constant wind.

## Transportation

### *Immediate:*
You *may* have an automobile that works in the first few weeks. However, gas stations will not be able to pump gas so the fuel in the tank is likely to be all you will have. Therefore, drive home immediately. If you work near your home, you can possibly walk. Expect massive traffic delays. If possible, try to leave ahead of everyone else at work and take alternate routes to avoid the traffic congestion that will surely happen. People who went through Hurricane Katrina spent literally hours on the highways to cover distances normally covered in one-tenth the time. *Do not stop along the way*.

### *Short-term / Medium-term to Long term:*
In the event you have a working vehicle, conserve fuel. Consolidate fuel from all sources (e.g., your mowers, garden equipment, motor bikes, and dirt bikes). If you have one of the few vehicles running, you may become a target for those who want your vehicle. *Do not stop to pick up "stranded" motorists.* They may be looking to take your vehicle.

In recent years, ex-military vehicles such as the time tested "deuce and a half" or "hummers" have been available to the civilian market. The "deuce"

---

will run on literally any fuel available and is extremely durable. But they also only get 10 miles per gallon!

Bicycles are another option. They are simple, silent, require little maintenance and can travel almost anywhere. Having several at your house is good planning. Also remember to have a lot of spare tire tubes, some tires and a mechanical pump or two.

If you live on a farm, diesel fuel may be available. Tractors aren't the best mode of transportation, but if you have a diesel-powered automobile, you may be able to use fuel from the tractor to power your car. Again, try not to advertise having fuel or a working vehicle.

"Bug Out Bags" are something to consider for your vehicle. They take up very little room and can be a lifesaver if needed. They can be stored in the trunk of the automobile. Following are links explaining what they are and suggested contents. There is a basic core of supplies, the rest is up to what you want, have room for, or meets your individual situation.

- Bug-out Bag[46]
- Bug Out Bag Academy[47]
- Urban Survival Bug Out Bag[48]
- Bug Out Bag Checklist[49]
- 12 Essential Survival Items Under $12[50]
- Best Prepper Resources and Recommendations[51]

---

[46]  https://en.wikipedia.org/wiki/Bug-out_bag
[47]  http://bugoutbagacademy.com/free-bug-out-bag-list/
[48]  http://www.amazon.com/Survival-Choose-Emergency-Disaster-Zone/dp/B00VS1RTBS
[49]  http://www.amazon.com/Survival-Choose-Emergency-Disaster-Zone/dp/B00VS1RTBS
[50]  http://graywolfsurvival.com/14778/12-essential-survival-items-under-12/
[51]  http://graywolfsurvival.com/95815/best-prepper-resources-and-recommendations-feb-2015/

The following chart was produced in 2012 by the American Transportation Association to show just how critical our nation's JIT (Just In Time) supply system is on the trucking industry. Compound this with the loss of everything electrical and the critical aspects of the problem become very clear.[52]

---

[52]   http://readynutrition.com/resources/when-the-trucks-stop-delivering-the-system-will-collapse_11072015/

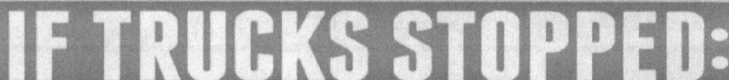

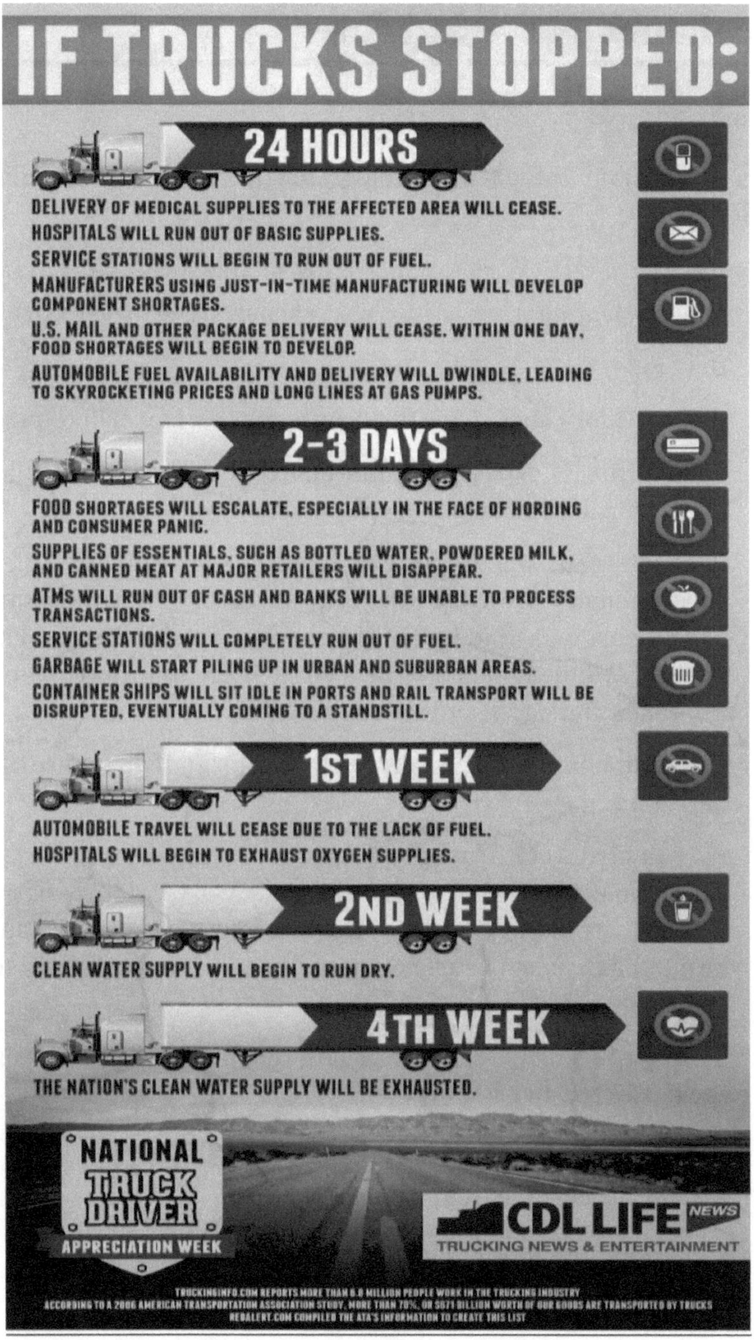
IF TRUCKS STOPPED:
24 HOURS
DELIVERY OF MEDICAL SUPPLIES TO THE AFFECTED AREA WILL CEASE.
HOSPITALS WILL RUN OUT OF BASIC SUPPLIES.
SERVICE STATIONS WILL BEGIN TO RUN OUT OF FUEL.
MANUFACTURERS USING JUST-IN-TIME MANUFACTURING WILL DEVELOP COMPONENT SHORTAGES.
U.S. MAIL AND OTHER PACKAGE DELIVERY WILL CEASE. WITHIN ONE DAY, FOOD SHORTAGES WILL BEGIN TO DEVELOP.
AUTOMOBILE FUEL AVAILABILITY AND DELIVERY WILL DWINDLE, LEADING TO SKYROCKETING PRICES AND LONG LINES AT GAS PUMPS.
2-3 DAYS
FOOD SHORTAGES WILL ESCALATE, ESPECIALLY IN THE FACE OF HORDING AND CONSUMER PANIC.
SUPPLIES OF ESSENTIALS, SUCH AS BOTTLED WATER, POWDERED MILK, AND CANNED MEAT AT MAJOR RETAILERS WILL DISAPPEAR.
ATMs WILL RUN OUT OF CASH AND BANKS WILL BE UNABLE TO PROCESS TRANSACTIONS.
SERVICE STATIONS WILL COMPLETELY RUN OUT OF FUEL.
GARBAGE WILL START PILING UP IN URBAN AND SUBURBAN AREAS.
CONTAINER SHIPS WILL SIT IDLE IN PORTS AND RAIL TRANSPORT WILL BE DISRUPTED, EVENTUALLY COMING TO A STANDSTILL.
1ST WEEK
AUTOMOBILE TRAVEL WILL CEASE DUE TO THE LACK OF FUEL.
HOSPITALS WILL BEGIN TO EXHAUST OXYGEN SUPPLIES.
2ND WEEK
CLEAN WATER SUPPLY WILL BEGIN TO RUN DRY.
4TH WEEK
THE NATION'S CLEAN WATER SUPPLY WILL BE EXHAUSTED.
NATIONAL TRUCK DRIVER APPRECIATION WEEK
CDL LIFE NEWS
TRUCKING NEWS & ENTERTAINMENT
TRUCKINGINFO.COM REPORTS MORE THAN 6.8 MILLION PEOPLE WORK IN THE TRUCKING INDUSTRY
ACCORDING TO A 2006 AMERICAN TRANSPORTATION ASSOCIATION STUDY, MORE THAN 70%, OR $671 BILLION WORTH OF OUR GOODS ARE TRANSPORTED BY TRUCKS
REDALERT.COM COMPILED THE ATA'S INFORMATION TO CREATE THIS LIST

# Miscellaneous

All timeframes

This is a "catchall" category for things not included above. Things to consider include:

1.  Hand tools. These will become very valuable, as they do not require power. Hammers, saws, pliers, wrenches, screwdrivers, drills, etc.

2.  Duct tape.

3.  Oils and lubricants. A working auto or generator will require oil.

4.  Games (this is especially important if you have small children). Cards can also be included.

5.  Books to read. One thought on books is the original Kindle. It is small enough it probably will not be affected. You can store around 3,000 books on a Kindle, many for medical, reference, or just novels to read. A Bible would also be a wise choice to include. The more reference and entertainment books, the better.

6.  Cigarette lighters will be very valuable for individual use and for bartering.

7.  Flashlights. Stock a lot of batteries or rechargeable batteries that can be maintained by a solar charger or even a solar flashlight. Lights using diodes are very bright, use very little energy and can be purchased very cheaply. Solar and hand-crank flashlights should also be included.

8.  Solar garden lights. These can charge during the day and be used in the evening. They are inexpensive.

9.  Wire in a spool. This can be useful for repairs, snares, etc.

10. A good supply of nails and screws of various sizes.

11. Something to store documents, e.g., marriage licenses, birth certificates, deeds for posterity.

12. Paper currency will very likely be worthless. One consideration is precious metals such as gold, silver or pre-1964 coins, which have high silver content. Smaller denominations are easier to use as currency.

13. Establishing a neighborhood network could provide a wide array of skills and resources. It can also assist in a defensive situation.

14. Purchase garden tools such as rakes, shovels, hoes, axes, and picks. On a farm they will be essential.

15. Although mentioned under **Food**, it would be wise to secure a large supply of heirloom seeds. Be selective and choose vegetables you like. They store easily and could be all the difference in your survival.

16. Writing materials for keeping records, communications or instructions.

17. Books on the skills and applications of the most recent pre-electric society will be essential. The need for this knowledge in establishing a life without electricity is critical. And, such skills could be used in bartering for services or other items.

18. Most ham operators have spare parts, wire, and connectors. If you are a ham operator and do not have this, now would be a good time to get some spares.

19. Alcohol and tobacco products will become like gold, literally. It would be wise to have a supply of each for bartering or trading. They both last a long time and do not deteriorate.

20. Rope/550 paracord.

21. Extra 2x4's or sheets of plywood for miscellaneous projects.

22. Nail clippers, scissors, razors, combs and other items for personal grooming.

23. As tragic as it is, people will die in a mass EMP/CME event. You may want to consider having plastic bags or rolls of plastic and shovels to address the issue of burying loved ones.

# Epilogue

What **YOU** can do to protect the grid.

Preparedness or Prevention?

## **Both**!

Rather than advocating the idea of prepping only one's self or ones family for a long-term blackout, the concept of community planning, hence the title of this monograph "Local Critical Task *Planning* for Long-Term Blackouts" is recommended. Taking the information contained within this manual to audiences outside of one's family and friends (i.e., local emergency planners, first responders, and community leaders) helps extend the pool of practitioners of Real Risk Management. It informs them of the NEED to plan and METHODS to plan for long-term outages. Most importantly, it provides a heightened level of awareness for the necessity to SECURE THE GRID.

The primary goal of the Secure the Grid Coalition[53] is to prevent long-term blackouts to the U.S. electric grid. We want to eliminate vulnerabilities to all hazards (physical attacks, cyber-attacks, nuclear EMP, and solar storms) and weaknesses in our national defense that invite hostility from adversaries. The Secure the Grid Coalition works on the "prevention" aspect of national security related catastrophes.

We caution people not to overemphasize an activity commonly known as 'prepping' because we do not believe people should *accept* the inevitability of a major blackout and therefore expend all of their time, energy, and resources on preparing for it. This is not to say citizens and local communities should not prepare for long-term outages; rather, people should not have the impression that if they just take care of themselves and their family that everything will be OK.

---

[53]  http://securethegrid.com/

When first responders and emergency planners realize their obligation to plan and prepare for long-term outages, this brings about an increased awareness among the policy makers who fund these entities. In an ideal world, America's legislators would have already applied Real Risk Analysis to laws that regulate the electrical industry and concluded, themselves, that there is an overwhelming need to secure the grid and plan for attacks on its infrastructure.

Success in securing America's electric grid will not come from the right law being passed or a minor shift in policy. It requires political leadership, scientific leadership, and public awareness; and a new level of sharing among scientific, engineering, and technological disciplines that informs policy makers and reforms regulatory capture.

The British government, for example, has a highly developed national preparedness plan for a major solar storm. Because they have acted responsibly on the preparation side, their government policy and electrical supply industry follow by implementing modern technologies that are resilient and less dependent on the old interconnected system.

Because the U.S. federal government has no significant preparedness plans for long-term blackouts, local first responders are beginning to develop emergency planning scenarios based on the EMP Commission's recommendations and are therefore the real leaders in protecting our nation's citizens.

## Who is taking action?

The Center for Security Policy, InfraGard, the Task Force on National and Homeland Security, the Foundation for Resilient Societies, EMPACT America, and High Frontier are diligently working on electrical grid vulnerability issues. Each organization can provide information about what they are doing and how you can get involved. The various battlefronts of engagement are as diverse as the groups making efforts to protect the grid and they include emergency planning, regulatory accountability, White House science policy, congressional affairs, missile defense, intelligence, space weather prediction, physical security, cyber security, industrial controls systems, nuclear power, and public education.

## The Center for Security Policy[54]
The Center for Security Policy has been involved in efforts to protect the electric grid for several years. In 2013, CSP formed the EMP Coalition, which evolved into the Secure the Grid Coalition,[55] as an "all hazards approach" to address other non-EMP (but equally devastating) threats to the grid. The Secure the Grid Coalition is a unique forum of scientists, engineers, intelligence professionals, and national security policy experts who are able to enhance insights about the electrical grid vulnerability by bridging gaps across their respective disciplines. In addition to the Secure the Grid Coalition, the Center for Security Policy works every day to inform lawmakers, legislators, and the public on threats to the electrical grid.

## InfraGard[56]
InfraGard is a partnership between the FBI and the private sector. It is an association of people who represent businesses, academic institutions, state and local law enforcement agencies, and other participants dedicated to sharing information and intelligence to prevent hostile acts against the U.S. It represents 17 categories of critical infrastructures and key resources. It also has an EMP Special Interest Group (SIG). The purpose of the InfraGard SIG is to address and mitigate the threat of a simultaneous nationwide collapse of infrastructure from any hazard such as manmade or natural EMP. Any threat that could cause a similar collapse of infrastructure over most or all of the U.S. is also of interest to the EMP SIG.

**The Task Force on National and Homeland Security**[57] is a privately funded and operated body with a Congressional mandate to educate and help protect the United States from the existential threat posed by a natural or manmade EMP catastrophe and other threats vital to U.S. national and domestic security that imperil the survival of the American people. Natural EMP from a great geomagnetic storm, a rare but highly probable threat that many scientists fear is overdue and may soon recur, could collapse electric grids worldwide and all the critical infrastructures (communications,

---

54    http://www.centerforsecuritypolicy.org/
55    http://securethegrid.com/
56    https://www.infragard.org/
57    http://www.emptaskforcenhs.com/

transportation, banking, finance, food and water) that sustain modern civilization and the lives of millions.

## Foundation for Resilient Societies[58]
The Foundation for Resilient Societies is dedicated to cost-effective protection of technologically advanced societies from infrequently occurring natural and man-made disasters. Their current area of emphasis is protection of the U.S. electric grid and also protection of nuclear power plants during long-term loss of outside commercial grid power. Their primary missions are scientific research and education; they are not a grass-roots membership-based organization. Their staff includes both technical and legal experts with dozens of years of experience in critical infrastructure protection and continuity of government issues. They distinguish themselves from other organizations by the depth of their technical and legal research.

## EMPACT America[59]
Empact America is a bipartisan, non-profit IRS 501(c)3 organization for citizens concerned about protecting the American people from a nuclear or natural EMP catastrophe.

## High Frontier[60]
The best way to deter and defend against an asymmetric or conventional HEMP (High Altitude EMP) attack is with a robust missile defense program. Ambassador Henry Cooper provides extensive educational resources on EMP threat tracking at www.highfrontier.org.

Exploring each of these groups and providing as much support in as many ways as possible moves America closer to solutions: Your involvement is essential.

---

[58]  http://www.resilientsocieties.org/
[59]  http://www.empactamerica.org/
[60]  http://highfrontier.org/

www.ingramcontent.com/pod-product-compliance
Lightning Source LLC
Chambersburg PA
CBHW030531290526
45786CB00004B/1678